A.D. 2006 Avoiding Doomsday

(Managing & Making the Most of Small to Medium Businesses)

by

Ian Hedley Bell

Bloomington, IN  Milton Keynes, UK

authorHOUSE®

AuthorHouse™
1663 Liberty Drive, Suite 200
Bloomington, IN 47403
www.authorhouse.com
Phone: 1-800-839-8640

AuthorHouse™ UK Ltd.
500 Avebury Boulevard
Central Milton Keynes, MK9 2BE
www.authorhouse.co.uk
Phone: 08001974150

First published by AuthorHouse 9/1/2006

ISBN: 1-4259-5275-5 (sc)

Printed in the United States of America
Bloomington, Indiana

This book is printed on acid-free paper.

PROLOGUE.

Whether a business is small, medium or large, the fundamentals of how to approach the management and projection of that business are much the same. The following text is not necessarily going to apply to all types of business and its prime objective is to bring to the reader's attention only the 'front line' specifics that need to be considered. This 'bible' is, therefore, an aide memoir from which to draw examples and concepts and to apply them to the business being considered.

There are, of course, many informed books on the market and some go into great depth as to the facts and data that they supply. This book has the secondary objective of offering a set of simple and basic facts that, at the end of the day, are those that will bring a business to success rather than failure. No reams of 'mumbo jumbo' text to confuse just simple straight forward facts in a logical order that will cut through the 'waffle' and give the reader what he wants to know – *straight up and simply expressed.*

Overriding any business is how it is perceived by both the market and the customer. It has often been said that *"Your best Inspector is the customer!"* Any business must produce the performance that will make it that much better than the next company and/or competitor. Remember the customer always has the choice of who he deals with.

> *"If you're going to make the market believe that you are that good, your record must show just that. This means via acceptable products or service which are advanced in concept, competitive in price, of acceptable quality and delivered on time! Failure to achieve any or all of the foregoing will be guaranteed to harm your future status."*

In any business, the prime overall objective must always be to:-

> *"Increase order intake, improve profit levels, spread the customer and product/service base and, therefore, enhance your market footprint."*

Whilst all areas of the business need to be reviewed, that does not necessarily mean that change for the sake of it should be implemented.

> *"SI FRACTUM NON SIT, NOLI ID REFIERE!"*

> *"IF IT AIN'T BROKE, DON'T FIX IT!"*

Contents

Appendices

CHAPTER 1.

KEY POINTS AND ISSUES IN STARTING AND RUNNING A BUSINESS.

Planning Ahead.

"I know what I want from my business – it's all clear in my mind, it's just a question of getting it down on paper so I've got something to work to."

Think ahead, plan how your business is going to take shape in the near term and where you want it to be in the longer term. Refer to your plan regularly and be prepared to change. Make your plan continue to suit your business. Feeling comfortable with it will make it easier for you to explain your objectives and ambitions to others.

Knowing Your Market.

"Giving your customer what they want – that's what it's really all about isn't it? A satisfied customer at the end of the day."

Ask yourself the question – "Why should anyone buy from me rather than a competitor?" If you can give reasons which are supported by facts, your business will stand a good chance of competing. Know your customers and what they want. Know your competitors and what they are doing. Take the time to research and understand your market – you may be missing out on opportunities that will give you a head start.

Pricing.

"I thought that I would start off by offering a really keen price so that I could build up sales, then I was going to increase my prices, but it didn't work…"

Take time to set your prices – they are a vital part of the equation which will make or break your business. Work out your break-even point and then look at your competitors' prices and the market in general. Be prepared to review what you charge on a regular basis. You are always best advised to think in terms of value rather than volume, that is, the quality of what you offer as opposed to how much you can sell.

Promotion and Selling.

Target your customers and think carefully about the way you present yourself to them - in everything that you do **be professional**. Choose the promotional activity most appropriate to your business but don't expect miracles over night – take note of what works and why, and what is less effective so as to reduce the risk of wasted effort.

Once you've won new business and a new customer, work hard to keep them happy so that you secure repeat business.

Staying in Control.

"I started out by following my business plan, but then I got too busy and well, things started to get out of control after that…."

Making a financial plan will help you to confirm the viability of your business. Maintaining it will give you the control you need to ensure that your business stays financially 'healthy' and it will help you to stay in control as your business develops. With regular reviews, it will show you if you are achieving your goals and enable you to take corrective action if necessary and in a timely manner.

CHAPTER 2.

THE STAGES OF BUSINESS.

"If you think that all of your problems are unique to your business, look around and ask other people in other businesses."

(a) General.

The development of a business falls basically into one of four phases.

SURVIVING.

CONSOLIDATION.

EARLY GROWTH.

TEAM BUILDING.

You could say that the phases equate to human life cycle from birth onwards. There is one important exception, however, in that a business can go backwards as well as forwards. An assessment of where the business is, with respect to the cycle, will allow you to decide which areas need to be worked on and developed.

(b) Survival (First six to twenty four months of business).

If you had an original Business Plan, it probably has little resemblance to the current 'actual' status.

A Business Plan is a "living document" and should be reviewed and amended as often as circumstances dictate.

This period is all about making a living and as profitably as possible.

(c) Consolidation.

As you emerge into this phase you should now have a clear view of what your business is, who are your customers and which suppliers (if applicable) can be relied upon.

At the same time you should also be aware of your weaknesses. These will probably be in management and business skills, rather than the 'core skills' required to provide your product or service.

This is the point where you will need to develop:-

- Good housekeeping attributes.
- Improved profit levels.
- Good administration and control of the business.
- Improved communication levels with the other members of the Team or Workforce.

(d) **Early Growth.**

The business should by now have a solid base on which to build. Time should now be available to plan for the future of the business rather than endure just a day to day existence.

You will need to be asking the following questions:-

- What are we?
- Where do we want to go?
- How are we going to get there?
- What are the implications for the business?

Can we also say what the business will look like in three years time?

These questions, or ones like them, are vital as one always needs to know why and what you are all about. In basic terms a business can only grow from three fundamental actions:-

1. Find more customers and develop your market.
2. Add to your product range or service offered.
3. Acquisition.

Growth is all about planning and to do that successfully, you must be in control!

(e) **Team Building.**

At this stage the business will be at a 'sophisticated' level and it is the point at which you need to build upon the skills of those around you.

The most important resource of all is **<u>TIME</u>** and the more efficient the use of it, the better the business will become!

You will need to evolve 'Line Management and Two Way Communication' and develop a good Management Style with strong leadership. How this can be achieved could take various paths but they are all basic and logical concepts.

CHAPTER 3.

WHO AM I?

"All business people learn by making mistakes – the wise ones learn from other people's mistakes."

"A professional approach is one whereby you might make a mistake once but never the same mistake twice!"

You need to assess, at whatever stage of your business, what your problems are as this is the first step to finding some solutions.

CHAPTER 4.

SURVIVING THE EARLY YEARS.

1. General.

Problems will arise from not preparing well enough in advance. Of course problems will always occur but it is imperative to **identify the cause, not the symptoms,** and to cure them as quickly and as efficiently as possible. If you only attack the symptoms, then relief will only be temporary and almost certainly the problems will return.

Check out your performance against the four problem areas:-

- Preparation.
- Unforeseen.
- Information.
- Strategic.

2. Preparation Problems.

(a) The Product or Service does not meet the customer's needs.
(b) You do not have enough customers to live on.
(c) Your Product or Service is different to that offered by your competitors.
(d) Reaching and attracting customers is proving difficult.
(e) You appear to be short of capital.
(f) You need more working capital than anticipated.
(g) Your cost and pricing policy is not right.
(h) Customers are taking too long to pay.
(i) Suppliers are proving to be unreliable.
(j) You planned for larger sales or over estimated production targets.
(k) You have too much or too little stock.
(l) You have weak technical or management skills.
(m) Communication with management and employees is difficult.

In the United Kingdom - The office of the Official Receiver lists the following, not in order of importance, as the most common reasons for a business to fail.

- Not enough capital.
- Not selling enough.
- Bad management.
- Taking too much cash from the business too early.
- Poor accounting.
- Lack of experience.

- Bad debts.
- Setting prices too low.
- Growing too quickly and running out of cash.
- Fraud.
- Operating costs getting out of hand.
- Poor supervision.
- Competition.

You can avoid virtually all of the above if you recognise them as potential problems from the start.

3. Unforeseen Problems.

Problems which are difficult to anticipate are:-

- Downturn in the economy.
- Key customers or suppliers let you down.
- Changes in the Law.
- Major changes in customer needs.
- Changes of key people e. g. Employees, Supplier, Bank Manager, etc.

All of the above are harder to overcome and usually need a reassessment of how the business should be run.

4. Information Problems.

Too often businesses concentrate on those areas generating money. The resultant is that you then tend to neglect monitoring your performance and analysing it. Problems which could cause extensive damage are then only sighted when it is too late!

You should instigate simple control systems to monitor:-

- Sales performance and customer feedback.
- Production – particularly in the efficient use of resources and control of waste and quality.
- Cash flow.
- Profit margins and the overall ability to make and sustain profits.

5. Strategic Problems.

The need to plan ahead and think strategically is very important. It does not always have to be a 'documented' plan; it can be just an attitude of mind.

Consider the following:-

- Try not to be dependent upon a single customer or supplier.
- Plan how to fund the business in the longer term.
- Keep in touch with the market in order to anticipate problems and spot opportunities.
- Solicit the views of key people such as customers, suppliers and even the Bank Manager.

Things you need to do regularly are:-

- Review the Business Plan with respect to market conditions.
- Continue to introduce and/or strengthen the basic system on which you rely.
- Learn how to analyse your performance thoroughly.
- Update your Business Plan whenever necessary.
- Increase the confidence, commitment and motivation of the workforce.

CHAPTER 5.

FOCUS AND DIRECTION.

"You would not consider starting out on a complicated vehicle journey without looking at a road map, so why run a business that way? Always have a clear view of where you want to go and how to get there!"

1. General.

Consider the following questions:-

Do you really know what your business is good at?

Do you have a good idea of where you want to be in three years?

Do you know if you are doing well enough to get there?

Simple enough questions you may think but **many, many** businesses fail to ask them.

The statement of a 'Busy Fool' – "I have more important things to do than plan!"

The Busy Fool works longer hours to achieve the same profit – or even less. The Busy Fool chases sales in the belief that turnover is the key to business success.

You are in 'the trap' if your turnover rises and your profits remain static or are falling. Remember that an increase in sales often leads to an increase in costs.

One target is to increase profitability but at least with the same turnover level. You will only be able to do this, however, if you analyse your performance and keep your finger on the pulse of the business.

Three main areas that you will need to review, in order to analyse performance, are:-

- Customers and markets.

- Finance – particularly cash and profits.

- Managing the operation – resources and people.

A SWOT (Strengths, Weaknesses, Opportunities & Threats) Analysis (See Appendix A) is a good simple way to start your planning.

2. Customers and Markets.

Irrespective of all of the "gobble de gook" you might be told or read, marketing is simply recognising the needs of present and potential customers and then meeting those needs.

Markets do not buy your goods – customers do!

Markets comprise many different 'segments' of customers and it is important that you recognise which type, in which segment, you want to do business.

The more you focus on the right segment, the more likely you are to be successful.

Ultimate success depends upon your customer perceiving that you offer something of better value than your competitors. You need to capitalise on your unique advantages.

Check your focus and direction by answering the following key questions:-

- Do you know the three main reasons why your customers buy from you?

- What are your business objectives and how often do you review progress?

- Which of your products or services earns the most and least profit?

- Where does the biggest potential in your business lie and why?

- Where would your customers buy if not from you?

- What significant changes have occurred in your business due to changes in economy?

You cannot be too frequent in your review of the focus and direction of your business.

The following is a list of attitudes and/or faults that exist within people who do not plan and, therefore, have little focus or direction!

> Being optimistic.
> Reading few business documents or trade journals.
> Only writing when you have to.
> Learn by doing things.
> Are inexperienced as a Manager.
> Are very independent.

The results of such traits are:-

- You will more than likely treat symptoms of problems instead of causes and the problems will return.

- You will always be throwing buckets of water on fires in stead of building a fire engine.

- You will not be certain as to where your business is going.

Success in winning business is as much to do with solving customer's problems as delivering a core product or service. If you get close to your customer you will be able to understand and solve their problems. To do this, however, you have to know what your core skills are and then to focus on them.

The underlying slogan is **"Know what you are good at and stick with it!"**

If you can ascertain why your customers buy from you, this will tell you what your competitive advantage is. Knowing what advantages you have will allow you to promote them in the market place.

CHAPTER 6.

FINANCE – PARTICULARLY CASH AND PROFIT.

"Cash is King! Many businesses fail because they run out of cash, even though they are profitable!"

1. General.

You must understand your accounts and how to relate them, as past or historical performances, to current and future activities.

Simple, quick and regular financial outputs are required to analyse performance. Fairly accurate information **now** is better than very accurate information that is out of date.

Five key marketing areas which make a successful business stand out are:-

1. Good at recognising and meeting customer needs.
2. Keeping nearly as much information on customer trends as for your own finances.
3. Knowing the markets and being aware of the wider issues that affect the business.
4. Understanding your customers via contact feedback with respect to products and services.
5. Integrating all of these elements together to make it easy for the customer to buy from you first.

In your business you should know:-

- The business's 'break-even point' and monitor sales against that point.
- The importance of 'gross margins'.
- How to manage cash flow.
- How to control fixed costs.

2. Managing the Operations.

Many businesses do not clearly know what is happening with respect to:-

Efficient use of machinery, time and space.
Standards of Quality.
Levels of waste.
The levels of performance necessary.

Simple standards need to be set and measured constantly. A well managed business should be that which sets out, monitors and meets standards, as they are applicable for:-

- The use of staff and equipment.
- Use of materials.
- Acceptable levels of rejects.
- Productivity hours available and used.
- Actual hours and materials used against those levels quoted for the job.
- Rework levels.
- Use of space.
- Sales for each person in relation to space available.
- Customer complaints.
- Work planning and delivery achievements.
- Theft/Stock that cannot be sold.

The key areas to look at will be those where performance is below the standards set. Continue to ask yourself:-

How well do I manage my operations?

Where are the key areas for improvements to be made?

How do I solve problems and make improvements?

3. Summary.

A business with clear focus and direction will be able to predict problems. Products and markets generally tend to go in cycles. That business which is able to see far enough ahead to predict the decline of a product or market and to do something about it is being well run.

You need to control your business, **not be controlled by it!** Four key questions to ask are:-

1. Where am I now?

2. Where do I want to be?

3. How am I going to get there?

4. What might get in my way?

Key areas which will help to make your business as effective as it can be are:-

- Making the best use of all of your assets.
- Using all of your resources efficiently.
- Meeting the highest levels of Quality.
- Keeping the waste of materials and time to a minimum.

CHAPTER 7.

YOURSELF AND THE MARKET.

"No customers – No business."

1. General.

Customers are your income, the better you are at dealing with customers, the more successful you will be.

Normally customers will buy from you because you provide more than the basic product or service. This is 'added value' and only the customer can decide what this means to him or his needs. He may buy from you for reasons you haven't even thought about. The only meaningful views are those of your customer and your task is to find out what they are.

The key is to get close to your customers and to build relationships. Customers will give you all of the important indicators about you, your product or service and even the competition. This will tell you why you stand out in a crowd as far as they are concerned.

To get this information you can either carry out a formal survey of your customer or ask them in conversation (See Appendix B – Customer Attitude Survey).

Once you know why your customers buy from you, you will then have a leader as to whom and where other potential customers might be. It is then a case of further analysis to ascertain in which segments of the market these customers exist.

A need for rationalisation of customers and products, in terms of turnover and profit, is a necessary regular exercise. It is a very well known fact that, in general, some 80% of a business comes from 20% of the customers or, put another way, 20% of the products generate 80% of sales. This is sometimes referred to as the '80:20 syndrome' and needs to be analysed thoroughly and used as a driver for the business.

Some of the things that can give added value are:-

- Quicker and more reliable service and delivery.

- Products or services that are not offered by others.

- Reputation.

- Strong 'after sales' service and support.

- Convenient location.

- Distinctive image.

- High quality products.

- Expertise and knowledge.

The only alternative to added value is to sell at a lower price than your competitors. However, if you reduce the price:-

- You will need to sell more.

- Your competitors may also produce at a lower price.

- A cheaper price may cause the thought that you are selling a poor product.

2. Sales Platform.

As well as knowing which products/services and which customer segments are the most profitable, you will need to generate enquiries. You will always need to seek out more potential customers than you sell to.

By analysing your promotional activities, you can asses what has attracted potential customers. This will give you an idea as to what your 'conversion rate' is for turning enquiries into orders and new customers. If you know how much business you want to do in a given time, you will then know how many potential customers you need to promote your business to.

Being able to do this is not hard; the method to use is a Sales Platform. Each business needs to generate its own Sales Platform. The following are two examples.

Example 1.

This is how a Kitchen Fitting company applied the technique.

			Source Information.
Step 1	Annual sales target.	£72,000.00	Business Plan target.
Step 2	Average order size.	£ 2,000.00	Previous experience.
Step 3	Orders needed each year.	36	Step 1 ÷ Step 2.
Step 4	Orders needed each month.	3	Step 3 ÷ 12.
Step 5	'Conversion Rate' – How many quotes become orders?	1 in 3	Previous experience or market intelligence.
Step 6	Number of quotes made each month.	9	Step 4 x Step 5.
Step 7	'Conversion Rate' – How many casual enquiries become quotes given?	1 in 6	Previous experience or market intelligence.
Step 8	Casual enquiries needed each month.	54	Step 6 x Step 7.

The monthly target for sales activities is, therefore, that 3 orders are needed to be completed, 9 quotes for new business have to be raised and 54 casual enquiries need to be attracted.

Example 2.

These are the figures of a Stationary Supplies business. The calculation considers 'repeat business' from existing customers as well as new business. The company sold £200,000.00 of stationary last year. Sales records showed 1,080 sales giving an average order value of £185.00. A close look at the sales records indicated that 972 of the orders were repeat business. So 90% of the firms business in any year was repeat.

$$\frac{(972 \times 100\%)}{(1,080)} = 90\%$$

To promote itself, the business visited potential customers in order to set up an opportunity to quote. Previous year's performance indicated that 3 sales visits generated 1 quote. Previous years records also indicated that for every 4 quotes generated, 1 order was received.

A sales target for the New Year was set at £250,000.00 and assuming that the average order size remained the same and some 90% of repeat orders being obtained.

			Source Information.
Step 1	Annual sales target	£250,000.00	Business Plan target.
Step 2	Average order size	£ 185.00	Previous records.
Step 3	Orders needed each year	1,351	Step 1 ÷ Step 2.
Step 3a	Orders that should come		

	from repeat business	1,216	Step 3 x 90%.
Step 3b	New orders needed in the year	135	Step 3 – Step 3a.
Step 4	Orders needed each month	11	Step 3b ÷ 12.
Step 5	'Conversion Rate' – How many quotes given become orders	1 in 4	Previous records.
Step 6	Number of quotes to be given each month	44	Step 4 x Step 5.
Step 7	'Conversion Rate' – How visits result in quotes	1 in 3	Previous records.
Step 8	Sales visits needed	132	Previous records.

Adaptable Sample Sheet.

			Source Information.
Step 1	Annual Sales Target	-	Business Plan target.
Step 2	Average order size	-	Previous records.
Step 3	Orders needed each year	-	Step 1 ÷ Step 2.
Step 3a	Orders that should come from repeat business	-	Previous records.
Step 3b	New orders needed in the year	-	Step 3 – Step3a.
Step 4	Orders needed each month	-	Step 3b ÷ 12.
Step 5	'Conversion Rate' – How many quotes given become orders	1 in ?	Previous records or research.
Step 6	Number of quotes that must be given each month	-	Step 4 x Step 5.
Step 7	'Conversion Rate' – How many potential customers visited result in a quote	1 in ?	Previous records or research.
Step 8	Potential customers you need to contact each month	-	Step 6 x Step 7.

The Sales Platform technique is a means of keeping sales activity 'driving' throughout the year and can be used for all types of business. It is also an excellent means of 'sighting' future problems. Always regularly check average order sizes and Conversion Rates as these point to the future success of the business.

Be aware that the success of your business depends upon "keeping your ear to the ground" in a number of ways. You need to know what is happening in the wider world, what your competitors are doing and what factors might affect your markets in the future.

There is a common belief that selling is about 'pressuring' the potential customer or 'manipulating' them – **<u>WRONG!</u>** Selling is about trading your human qualities. Research shows that 83% of customers like the sales person they have been dealing with. This is another concept of added value!

The following is a list of things that have been shown to have a major impact on businesses in recent years.

- Economic trends.
- Increase in the demand for Quality such as ISO 9000, BS5750 and the like.
- The ageing of the population.
- 'Green' issues.
- Higher customer expectations.
- Changes in Regulations and the Law.

Potential customers will trust you if:-

- You keep your promises.

- You get to meetings on time.

Some companies have employed 'Sales Prevention Officers!' This being by adopting a manner and style which upsets customers. **<u>This person WILL prevent sales! Have you got one?</u>**

Successful sales people are those that listen to the customer, not just talk to him. Two thirds of the message that you put across is via 'body language.' Be positive and enthusiastic, make it obvious that you are listening and take notes. At the end of a meeting, go back over the discussion and summarise the main points.

Always try to be prepared for customer negative points or objections. Some will crop up regularly so allow for a degree of 'rehearsal' of your answer.

Because you are not hearing of complaints does not mean that they do not exist! As much as 68% of buyer/seller relationships change because the customer feels indifferent to the supplier. In general people do not complain, they just go elsewhere.

If you do not put the same effort into keeping customers as winning them, then they will walk away. Worse than that, they will tell some 10 other people about their bad experience (normally good experiences are only passed on to 5 people, at most!). Keep in touch with your customer for the bad points; even more than for the good!

Being positive and 'customer orientated' sets a really good successful business above the rest.

At Appendix C is a 'Marketing Effectiveness Questionnaire' that will help decide how to 'customer orientate' your business. It is designed to help you look at your own business.

Never criticise your competitors in front of a current or potential customer. Your competitors do a good job but you can do better!

CHAPTER 8.

CASH AND PROFIT.

"The business only took off when I understood the difference between cash and profit."

1. General.

Cash and profit are not the same. Profitable businesses can run out of cash and businesses can be temporarily 'cash rich' without being profitable.

Whether referring to cash or profit, however, they are both equally important. Ensuring that you receive monies owed, before you spend it, is managing your cash effectively which, in essence, means ensuring that your prices are right and your costs are controlled.

There are two key elements to profitability. Making the correct gross profit margin and controlling the actual fixed costs of the business.

2. Managing Finances.

Good quality information is required to ensure that you are:-

- Pricing products and/or services at the right level for the market.

- Maintaining a suitable profit margin.

Appendix D illustrates a number of 'Useful Calculations'(financial ratios) that will help assess the performance of your business.

Appendices E and F illustrate Operating Budget and Cashflow Forecasts respectively and compare actual performance against budget.

3. Pricing.

A big mistake commonly made is to believe that all customers will pay the same 'rate' for the job! All jobs are different and should be priced according to the surrounding issues and complexities. It is, however, important to work out an average price for your product or service that you need to maintain each year.

The calculation of this average price for your product or service is fairly simple:-

1. Work out your overheads.
2. Decide how much personally you wish to take out of the business.

3. Assess the tax you are likely to pay.
4. Estimate how many 'saleable' hours or days you have and that your employees can work.

Average Price = $\dfrac{(1 + 2 + 3)}{4}$

If the average price equates to higher than the market price will pay, your business has no future unless you can alter the base calculation components. It should also be noted that it would be above the norm to be able to utilise more than 50% of the total hours available.

4. **Information.**

The basis of all business decisions is good information. The better the information, the better your ability to make the right decisions.

Information must be gathered and checked frequently (at least once a month) against forecast. The secret of good financial management is to use historic performance information to steer yourself into the future.

At Appendix G is a simple Financial Problem Diagnostic Chart.

5. **Break-even Point.**

Always keep a regular break-even chart as it is a good way of monitoring how profitable your business is.

Break-even Point = $\dfrac{\text{Fixed Cost (Regardless of level of sales)}}{\text{Gross Profit Margin}}$

(a) *Working out your Break-even Point.*

Break-even is the level of sales you need to cover all of your fixed costs (both fixed and variable). Here is how some Fibreglass Manufacturers worked out their break-even point. The same calculations apply to any business.

Forecast over the next 12 months.

1. Sales	£108,000.00
2. Opening stock	£ 38,000.00
3. Plus purchases	£ 60,000.00
4. Less closing stock	£ 50,000.00
5. Goods or materials used (2 + 3) – 4	£ 48,000.00

6. Wages and salaries	£ 32,000.00	
7. Fixed costs	£ 10,360.00	

From these figures you can work out your projected gross and net profit. That is to say, your profit before (gross) and after (net) you have allowed for fixed costs.

1.	Sales	£108,000.00
5.	Goods or materials used (2 + 3) – 4	£ 48,000.00
6.	Wages and salaries	£ 32,000.00
8.	Less variable costs (5 + 6)	£ 80,000.00
9.	Gross profit (Profit before fixed costs) [1 - 8]	£ 28,000.00
7.	Less fixed costs	£ 10,360.00
10.	Net profit (Profit after fixed costs) [9 – 7]	£ 17,460.00

Now you need to work out your gross profit margin. This is your profit before allowing for fixed costs. It is written as a percentage of sales.

$$\frac{\text{Gross Profit} \times 100}{\text{Sales}} = \frac{28,000.00 \times 100}{108,000.00} = 25.9\%$$

If you can reach the gross profit margin and your fixed costs do not change, the break-even turnover is worked out as follows:-

$$\frac{\text{Fixed Costs} \times 100}{\text{Gross Profit Margin}} \quad = \quad \frac{10,360 \times 100}{25.9} \quad = \quad £40,000.00$$

Therefore, this business will need a turnover of £40,000.00 to cover all fixed costs, as long as it keeps the same gross profit margin.

Looked at another way...............

£40,000.00 turnover at 25.9% gross profit margin = £10,360.00.

This is just enough to cover the fixed costs.

Finally work out the amount you need to sell every month to break-even. This figure is important because you can use it to check whether or not you are on target, or need to make some adjustments. But remember that this calculation does not take into account any seasonal changes that might affect your business.

To work out the monthly target, simply take your break-even sales figure for the year and divide by twelve.

$$\frac{40,000.00}{12} = £3,333.33$$

Using the annual break-even figure, a very simple but informative graph (See Appendix H – Breakdown Graph) can be produced to show how profitable (or not) your business is over a particular period. There is a straight line representing the Break-Even point at the end of twelve months which is £40,000.00. At the end of each month you would plot your Actual Sales on the same graph. In the example shown all plots are drawn as a straight line for simplicity but, in reality, this would be very unlikely. If the Expected Sales target of £108,000.00 is achieved at the gross profit margin of 25.9% and plotted on the example, it can be seen that the business would be highly profitable. However, if the business only achieved sales of £30,000.00 (as the example also shows) the business would be showing a loss. In such latter circumstances, the business could only recover and survive by increasing sales or improving the profit margin.

The higher you can work above the break-even point, the greater your margin of profit and, more importantly, your safety. One of the most sensitive items in your break-even analysis is your gross profit margin (Profit before taking off fixed costs).

(b) **Gross Profit Margin.**

Achieving or bettering your gross profit margin is of vital importance. Compare it with the calculations you made at the start of the year. When the gross margin falls below what you expect, the effect on your business can be devastating. The typical reaction to difficult trading conditions or poor performance is to reduce prices to try to increase sales volume. This causes you to have to put in more work for less return, as shown in the following charts.

Chart A shows the extra business needed to be generated to make the same gross profit if you reduce your prices. In the Fibreglass Manufacturers examples, they had a gross profit margin above 25%. If they decided to reduce their selling prices by 10%, they would need to generate 67% more sales to compensate for the price reduction.

On the other hand, Chart B shows what volume of business you can afford to loose if you put your prices up. The same Fibreglass Manufacturers can now afford to loose 29% of their existing volume of business, if they increase their prices by 10%.

Chart A – *The negative effect of reducing your price – Sales have to increase hugely for you to remain profitable.*

Existing % Gross Margin.

% Price Reduction	5	10	15	20	25	30	35	40	50
	% Volume increase required for the same gross profit								
2.0	67	25	15	11	9	7	6	5	4
3.0	150	43	25	18	14	11	9	8	6
4.0	400	67	36	25	19	15	13	11	9
5.0		100	50	33	25	20	17	14	11
7.5		300	100	60	43	33	27	23	18
10.0			200	100	67	50	40	33	25
15.0				300	150	100	75	60	43

Chart B – *The positive effect of increasing your price –Sales can decrease sharply and yet you remain profitable.*

Existing Gross Margin.

% Price Increase	5	10	15	20	25	30	35	40	50
	% Volume decrease to generate the same gross profit								
2.0	29	17	12	9	7	6	5	5	4
3.0	37	23	17	13	11	9	8	7	6
4.0	44	29	21	17	14	12	10	9	7
5.0	50	33	25	20	17	14	12	11	9
7.5	60	43	33	27	23	20	18	16	13
10.0	67	50	40	33	29	25	22	20	17
15.0	75	60	50	43	37	33	30	27	23

This is why businesses get sucked into a spiral of 'decline and failure' during difficult times. They cut prices believing that they have to maintain turnover. As we can see, this action has a huge effect on gross profit – sales have to go up to compensate. Often, the most difficult thing to do is to increase sales. And when the necessary increase in sales does not happen, many businesses react by reducing prices yet again – another loop in the spiral to failure! A good business will try to reach a better gross margin. **Profit is the key to business, not sales!**

"TURNOVER IS VANITY, PROFIT IS SANITY BUT CASH FLOW IS REALITY!"

Before reducing your price, check your current gross margin percentage. Next, read across the relevant 'price reduction' line in Chart A to find out what percentage increase in sales you would need, to make the same gross profit. Then use Chart B to asses whether increasing your price, to achieve the gross margin from reduced sales, is a more realistic option.

Always remember:-

* Be realistic about how much work you can do.
* When working out your prices, take into account hours and days that you cannot

charge your customer for.
- Increasing sales without increasing profits makes you a *'busy fool!'*

(c) <u>Debtors and Creditors.</u>

If you pay your bills faster than your customers pay you, your business will need more cash. However long you give your customers to pay, you must chase your debtors for money when it becomes overdue. You depend upon payment from customers to run your business, you cannot afford customers who are bad payers!

If a customer is consistently late in paying, you will have to ask yourself if you can really afford to have him as a potential to destroy your business. Likewise, if you treat your suppliers badly, do not be surprised if they decide not to do business with you. Reliable suppliers are just as important as happy customers.

A 'debtor matrix' is a helpful way to monitor the speed at which your debtors pay their bills. At the end of each month, add up how much your debtors owe you and how long each bill has been unpaid. Use this information to complete a 'debtor matrix.' An example of this is as follows below.

Debtor Matrix.

Amount Owing (£'s).

Debtor	Total	<30 Days	30 – 60 Days	60 – 90 Days	>90 Days
1A	1,000.00	500.00	500.00		
2B	1,000.00	0	1,000.00		
3C	5,000.00	2,000.00	500.00	3,500.00	
4D	1,500.00	1,500.00	0		
5E	4,000.00	0	4,000.00		
6F	4,000.00	4,000.00	0		
7G	0	0	0		
8H	1,000.00	0	1,000.00		
9I	8,000.00	3,000.00	2,000.00	2,000.00	1,000.00
10J	2,000.00	1,000.00	1,000.00		
Total	28,000.00	12,000.00	10,000.00	5,500.00	1,000.00

Remember that every 30 days debts that remain unpaid move into the next column. A blank Debtor Matrix is given at Appendix I.

COMMON CAUSES OF CASH & PROFIT PROBLEMS.

1. You allow your customers too long to pay their bills.
2. You keep too much stock.
3. You are paying your bills too quickly.
4. You are taking too much out of the business.
5. You have spent too much on equipment.
6. Your business is short of capital.
7. Your relationship with your bank could be better.
8. You are not meeting your sales targets.
9. Your overheads are too high.
10. You have lost control of your profit margins.
11. You are spending too much on your materials.
12. Your labour costs are too high.
13. You are selling unprofitable products or services.

CHAPTER 9.

MANAGING YOUR RESOURCES.

"Resources are scarce and time is money – make sure that you use both efficiently and effectively."

1. General.

The key thing is to manage your resources wisely. It is a fact that there is both 'income generating' time as well as 'non income generating' time and both are equally as important. The latter is composed of items involved with the planning and administration of the business and as such has to be taken into account when evolving a pricing policy.

2. Managing Time.

Having already looked at focus and direction, it is important to make sure that your activities move you in the right direction. Time is one of your most valuable resources and it is important to manage and prioritise it.

- Prime or priority time.
- Next order time.
- Less essential time.

Plan your days in order of importance i. e. **PLAN AHEAD!** Always remember to ask yourself "Is what I am doing now making the best use of my time?"

Get your time management right and structured around your major aims! Work harder yes – but make sure that you work wisely.

3. Managing Stocks and Assets.

The quicker you turn over your stock, the more efficiently the investment is working for you! Too much or too little stock will make your business less profitable and less efficient.

In managing your assets, look to the four key issues of – **use, efficiency, quality and waste.** From information gathered, decide:-

- How well the product side of your business is managed.
- Where there are key areas for improvement.

If you have a business that has very little stock, your time and the 'saleable time' of your staff become even more important with respect to efficient management.

CHAPTER 10.

MANAGING YOUR BUSINESS RELATIONSHIPS.

"Managing a business is all about working contacts and maintaining relationships with a wide range of people."

1. General.

You will need to find the time to develop the right relationships with all of the key people who come into contact with your business i. e. Bank Manager, Customers, Employees, etc. At the same time you will need to form a wider network of contacts who may well become 'key people' too.

Each relationship will be different and will need to be balanced by the nature of the interface. In essence, the parts that are played by various people are:-

How key people contribute to the business.

Existing Customers	**Income, market, information on new sales.**
Potential Customers	**Future income and market information.**
Suppliers/Sub contractors/ Competitors	**Goods and services and information.**
Staff	**Promote the business ideas.**
Agents and Distributors	**Sales opportunities and ideas.**
Competitors	**Motivation to improve.**
Bank Manager	**Financial support.**
Professional Advisers	**Extra skills.**

2. Delegation.

Line Management and Communication is both important and a **'two way street.'** The rules to follow are very simple:-

- Decide which task you wish to delegate (make sure that you concentrate on the key business issues).
- Discuss with the person to do the task, its nature and objective and ensure that they have all that is necessary to do it.
- Agree a timescale of when the task is to be completed.
- Let the person get on with the task, don't interfere but monitor and encourage!

Proper delegation is an essential part of good management, **abdication is not**!

You are a major influence on your staff, so use it to your advantage or you will become a victim of it. Lead by example (As any good Captain should), you are a 'role model' so don't expect them to do things that you don't do yourself.

Give genuine praise where it is deserved as it can never be enough and it will increase productivity. Talk to poor performers in a positive manner using questions such as:-

You are better than this aren't you?

How can we get it right next time?

What have you learned from this?

CHAPTER 11.

WHERE TO NEXT?

"Sustainable business growth is controlled and planned in a way that reduces unpleasant surprises."

A business's rate of growth over a period of time and the accompanying changes will be reflected in the way that the business is managed. Most businesses grow in a most haphazard manner because they have **no plan!** For growth to be effective, it must be done in planned phases as a result of defined management actions.

Growth usually requires an associated increase in working capital. A good rule of thumb is to fund at least 50% from profits retained in the business.

It is virtually impossible to stop a business growing. A business that is not going forwards is more than likely to be going backwards. If the rest of the world keeps moving and you stand still, you will become out of date, behind the market and competition and eventually out of the running. Remember always the four key questions:-

1. **Where am I now?**
2. **Where do I want to be?**
3. **How am I going to get there?**
4. **What might get in my way?**

Growth can be measured in the size of the increase in several areas and each can indicate a different type of growth. They include:-

- **Profit.**
- **Value of the business.**
- **Turnover.**
- **Number of employees.**
- **Value added/return on capital employed.**
- **Levels of production.**

APPENDIX A.

SWOT ANALYSIS.

Business name:

Strengths	Weaknesses

Opportunities	Threats

APPENDIX B.

CUSTOMER ATTITUDE SURVEY.

General.

This is a step by step method to help carry out a Customer Attitude Survey, the procedure used is both tried and tested and can be used by phone, e-mail or mail shot.

Step 1.

Identify some customers, including:-

- Customers who give you most of your sales.
- Customers you have lost.
- Customers you would like to do more business with in the future.

Aim for 10 to 30 contacts in total (or more if you have a large customer base).

Step 2.

Write the following to your customer:-

Dear X,

To help us asses and improve the overall standard of our service/products, we are carrying out a brief customer survey.

To do this, we are asking our customers for their opinions and advice on our service/products. We will, therefore, be phoning you soon regarding this matter.

It won't take up much of your time and we would be very grateful for your views.

Thank you for your help.

Yours sincerely,

Step 3.

Decide what information you need and design your questions. For example, here are some that could be asked:-

- What do you look for in a supplier (Ask for specific details)?
- What disappointments you about suppliers?

- What improvements could we make in our service to you?
- How often do you like suppliers to contact you?
- How could we do more business with you in the future?

You can design your own questions or change them into your own words. Each question can be followed up with questions asking for greater details such as follows:-

- Can you give me an example?
- Exactly what do you mean by that?
- What other things are important to you?

Step 4.

Make sure that the person you use to phone is 'comfortable' speaking with customers over the phone and is a good listener.

Set out your questions and write the customers name on each form. Ensure that the questions are adhered to word for word and that the answers are done the same – not an interpretation! Ask open questions and not those that can be answered by Yes or No. If the survey is done professionally and properly it will improve your image with the customer.

Step 5

Phone the customer some 3 days after sending them the letter. Ask them to identify which are the most important issues in Step 3. Then take each of them in turn and ask them to rate your business on a scale of 1 – 5, with 1 = Awful and 5 = Excellent.

> For example:-"Mr. Customer, you said that delivery was your number two priority. On a scale of 1 – 5, where do you rate us? Do you mind if I ask whether our major competitors are above or below that rating?

Step 6.

Assess the information collected. Which issue was mentioned most frequently? What are your customers' most important needs? How do they see your business?

You should end up with a list of customer needs and a rating of your performance compared to your competitors.

Clearly the next step is to take **action** to build on your strengths and deal with important weaknesses. You may also have identified some new opportunities in your research which you now want to take up.

Businesses are sometimes worried that customers will not talk enough or will not be honest.

You will probably find that the problem is not getting people to talk but stopping them talking. Remember, they are far more used to sales persons trying to sell to them than people genuinely interested in their views.

Step 7.

Consider following up your survey by thanking the customers that took part by phoning or by letter. You may even wish to tell them some of the results and how you will be changing or improving what you offer.

APPENDIX C.

MARKETING EFFECTIVENESS QUESTIONNAIRE.

General.

The Marketing Effectiveness Questionnaire is designed to assess how 'customer orientated' your business is. It won't tell you what you need to do to improve but it can suggest marketing strengths in your business and areas that might need some improvement.

Base your answers on *your assessment* of your marketing effectiveness (not what you believe is your customers' assessment). Tick the answer that is most appropriate to your business.

Major attribute – Customer philosophy.

1. Do you recognise the importance of designing the business to serve the needs and wants of particular markets?

    a. We sell to whoever will buy.
    b. We sell to specific market segments.
    c. Yes, we analyse customer needs and serve specific segments.

2. Do you develop different products or services and marketing plans for different segments of the market?

    a. Occasionally.
    b. Never.
    c. Quite often.

3. Have you developed any advantages over your main competitors that attract customers?

    a. We concentrate on selling the brand name or 'British Made' or competing on price.
    b. We concentrate on providing superior quality goods and services, guaranteed reliability or unmatched customer service.
    c. We have not developed any advantages over our main competitors.

Major attribute – Developing business.

4. How much effort do you put into building the business for the future?

    a. None. We concentrate on servicing existing customers – profit is what counts.
    b. Some effort.

    c. We go for a balance between short-term and long-term.

5. How experienced and effective are your sales persons?

    a. Very experienced, able to achieve one sale for every two opportunities (1:2).
    b. Some experience. All right with existing customers but does not relish cold calls.
    c. No experience, dislike selling.

6. How effective is your advertising and promotion in generating leads and enquiries?

    a. More leads than we can cope with.
    b. Some leads but not enough.
    c. We have to work very hard to find leads.

Major attribute – Proper marketing information.

7. When did you last carry out marketing research studies of your customers, their buying influences and your competitors?

    a. Several years ago (over 5 years or never).
    b. A few years ago (1 to 5 years).
    c. Recently (within the last few months).

8. How well do you know the sales and profit potential of different market segments, customers, sales areas, products and order sizes?

    a. Very well – we have detailed analysis and research.
    b. Quite a bit – we have information on certain parts.
    c. Not at all.

9. How effective is your marketing information system at providing high quality data quickly and accurately to help marketing decisions?

    a. Very effective information system, constantly updated and used.
    b. Quite effective system – but sometimes not fast, accurate or complete enough to help.
    c. We have no system – we rely on gathering information informally or by intuition.

Major attribute – Planning strategy.

10. What is the extent of your marketing planning?

    a. We develop a detailed annual marketing plan and careful long term plans that we monitor and update.
    b. We develop a formal marketing plan.

    c. We do little or no formal marketing planning.

11. What is the quality of your current marketing strategy?

    a. The current marketing strategy is not clearly defined.
    b. The current strategy is clear and just extends our past strategy.
    c. The current strategy is clearly defined and well reasoned with new ideas.

12. What are the main marketing objectives?

    a. To achieve short term profits and maintain our present position.
    b. To dominate the market by significantly increasing our share of the market and growing aggressively.
    c. No real strategic long term objectives.

Major attributes – Marketing efficiency.

13. What is your precise policy and how effective is it?

    a. We charge what we can get.
    b. We charge the same or less than our competitors.
    c. We charge more than our competitors to match the high quality of our product or service.

14. What marketing techniques do you regularly use to improve business performance?

    a. We do not use marketing techniques. We just assess our past performance.
    b. We regularly use a wide range of marketing techniques, including sales platform and customer attitude surveys.
    c. We have some marketing techniques that we use when necessary.

15. How effective is your marketing compared to that of your major competitors?

    a. An outsider would regard us as better than our competitors.
    b. We are about the same as our competitors.
    c. Frankly, we are not as good at marketing as our competitors.

Scoring System.

Add up the marks for your answers to each question.

Question	Box	Marks	Total of marks per question.
1.	a.	0	
	b.	1	
	c.	2	
2.	a.	1	
	b.	0	
	c.	2	
3.	a.	1	
	b.	2	
	c.	0	
4.	a.	0	
	b.	1	
	c.	2	
5.	a.	2	
	b.	1	
	c.	0	
6.	a.	2	
	b.	1	
	c.	0	
7.	a.	0	
	b.	1	
	c.	2	
8.	a.	2	
	b.	1	
	c.	0	
9.	a.	2	
	b.	1	
	c.	0	
10.	a.	2	
	b.	1	
	c.	0	
11.	a.	0	
	b.	1	
	c.	2	
12.	a.	2	
	b.	1	
	c.	0	
13.	a.	1	
	b.	0	
	c.	2	

14.	a.	0
	b.	2
	c.	1
15.	a.	2
	b.	1
	c.	0

Total

1. Analysis of results.

Major attributes	Score
Customer philosophy	................/6
Developing business	................/6
Proper marketing information	................/6
Planning strategy	................/6
Marketing efficiency	................/6
Total score	................/30

2. Evaluation of results.

2.1 Marketing effectiveness.

0 – 5	6 – 10	11 – 15	16 – 20	21 - 25	26 – 30
None	Not very effective	Fair	Good	Very good	Very Effective

2.2 Areas for action.

Even if you scored highly, there should still be scope for improvement. Maybe the questionnaire has given you some ides for actions to improve your business.

APPENDIX D.

USEFUL CALCULATIONS.

General.

This appendix contains some of the key indicators used by businesses to keep track of their performance.

Background.

It is often difficult to look at a profit and loss account or balance sheet and get a full picture. Because of this, ratios are often used to interpret accounts. A ratio is simply a relationship between two numbers. It indicates how a business is performing and can show trends and patterns when compared to the same ratios for previous years and to those of similar businesses. No single ratio should be relied on in isolation. Most types of businesses have typical ratios which can be used as a bench mark (sometimes called 'industry norms.').

There are four different types of financial ratio:-

1. **Liquidity – how much working capital you have.**
2. **Solvency – how near the business is to bankruptcy.**
3. **Efficiency – how good the management is.**
4. **Profit – how good the business is as an investment.**

Each type of ratio, and what it can tell you about your business, is described below.

1. Liquidity Ratio.

A business should normally have enough current assets (such as stock, work in progress, debtors and cash) to cover current liabilities (such as an overdraft and creditors). Liquidity ratios show the ability to meet your liabilities with the assets you have. The 'current ratio' shows the relationship of current assets to current liabilities.

$$\text{Current Ratio} = \frac{\text{Current Assets}}{\text{Current Liabilities}}$$

This should usually be between 1.5 and 2. If less than 1 (so that current liabilities are more than current assets), it means that the amount of working capital you have may become an area of concern – you may be relying on bank borrowing or delaying paying creditors to finance your trading.

You may possibly be relying on another source of finance for your daily operating expenses. If it is not between 1 and 2, it doesn't necessarily mean that your business is run badly, but it could be a dangerous sign. You might ask, for example, how pressing your creditors or the bank are for repayment, and if you are generating enough money to meet these liabilities?

If it is over 2, you may not be making the best use of your current assets. You need to Make sure that you are:-

- Making the best use of your cash.
- Not holding too much stock.
- Not letting debtors get out of hand.

A stricter test of liquidity is where current assets, that could be hard to sell, such as stock and work in progress, are not included. The remaining current assets of debtors and cash (or 'quick assets') are compared with current liabilities to give a 'quick ratio.'

$$\text{Quick Ratio} = \frac{\text{Quick Assets}}{\text{Current Liabilities}}$$

This should normally be around 0.7 to 1, although this can depend upon the industry. If the current ratio is rising and the quick ratio is static, you may have too many debtors.

It can be helpful to work out the number of days that the business can exist if no more cash flows into it. This is called a 'defensive interval' – as a guide, it should be 30 to 90 days, though it also depends on what industry your business is in.

$$\text{Defensive Interval} = \frac{\text{Quick Assets}}{\text{Daily Operating Expenses}}$$

Finally the Net Working Asset ratio shows the working capital that a business needs to support sales:-

$$\text{Net Working Assets} = \frac{(\{\text{Stock} + \text{Debtors}\} - \text{Creditors}) \times 100}{\text{Sales}}$$

It shows how much working capital you need for every £100.00 of your sales. Usually this would need to come from cash or bank borrowing, so this ratio can be useful for estimating how much extra cash you would need to finance an increase in sales.

2. Solvency Ratios.

If your total liabilities are more than total assets, then your business is technically insolvent. That means that if your business closed, it would not be possible to repay all of the people you owe money to. Allowing a business to trade whilst being insolvent is an offence (Certainly by Law in the United Kingdom), so you need to watch these figures closely.

The ratio of the money that you have borrowed (for example, loans, overdrafts and hire purchase) to the total capital of the business ('owners' or 'shareholders' capital and reserves) will show the 'gearing' of the business. Generally, the more money you borrow, the higher the gearing.

$$\text{Gearing} = \frac{\text{Total Borrowing}}{\text{Total Capital}}$$

Gearing is important in assessing how much the business can afford to borrow. A well established rule of thumb is that a bank would not normally like to have more money in a business than the owners have themselves invested, at least until it can demonstrate its success. This is because a bank's money is not its own to lend and there must be a good certainty of getting it back. However, exceptions are often made for new businesses or in other special circumstances.

Also if your cash flow and profits are stable you can afford higher gearing. Profits kept in the business add to your stake in the business and, therefore, increase your ability to borrow safely. Losses worsen gearing and make the business vulnerable and because of this another measure to use with gearing is your profit compared with the interest on your loans, or 'interest cover.'

$$\text{Interest Cover} = \frac{\text{Profit before Interest and Tax}}{\text{Interest}}$$

This shows how easily you will be able to pay interest on any borrowings. If it is over 4 it is very good, if it is under 2.5, however, it might show that you could have a problem if interest rates go up.

3. **Efficiency Ratios.**

These show how much working capital is being used, how quickly you can collect unpaid debts and pay your creditors, and how effective you are in controlling stock and making your cash work for you. The first ratio tells you the number of times unpaid debts are 'turned over.'

$$\text{Debtor Turnover Ratio} = \frac{\text{Sales}}{\text{Debtors}}$$

Ideally, use the average debtors for a particular period. You can estimate this by dividing sales by debtors at then end of a given period.

If you divide this ratio into the days of the year, you can get an annual based collection period for the number of days to collect debts.

$$\text{Debtor Collection Period} = \frac{365 \times \text{Debtors}}{\text{Sales}}$$

You need to keep tight control of your debtors. Keep the collection period as short as you can. Some businesses offer 30 days but often it can be far worse than that. Again, it depends upon the business that you are in.

Monitoring how long it takes you to pay your suppliers is as important as knowing how long your customers take to pay you. If suppliers have to wait too long, they may withdraw your credit. For this purpose, use the 'creditor turnover ratio.'

$$\text{Creditor Turnover Ratio} = \frac{\text{Sales}}{\text{Creditors}}$$

As with the Debtors Turnover Ratio, you can divide this ratio into the days of the year to get an 'average payment period.'

$$\text{Creditor Payment Period} = \frac{365 \times \text{Creditors}}{\text{Sales}}$$

Normally, the cost of sales is used to calculate the average payment period. It can be interesting to compare your business with another one, and you can do this by estimating your competitors' cost of sales.

Ideally, your average creditor payment period should be more than your average debtor collecting period. Otherwise, you're paying the money that you owe before you get the money for what you've sold, and you will probably find that your business will be short of cash.

Stock will increase when you are expanding and decrease when you are shrinking. For some businesses, such as wholesalers and sometimes retailers, a high 'stock turnover ratio' is essential to make any profit. Again, the level of stock will depend upon the industry that you are in. A low stock turnover ratio might show that the stock is moving slowly, which means that measures may need to be taken to dispose of it.

$$\text{Stock Turnover Ratio} = \frac{\text{Cost of Sales}}{\text{Average Stock at Cost}}$$

How quickly the stock 'turns' or is sold is another helpful figure.

$$\text{Average Holding Period} = \frac{365 \times \text{Average Stock at Cost}}{\text{Cost of Sales}}$$

4. Profit Ratios.

There are a number of simple ratios that show how profitable you are. The 'gross profit margin' is one figure that you should watch closely. It is probably the most important of all ratios as a pointer that your business is going 'off track' or not.

$$\text{Gross Profit Margin} = \frac{\text{Gross Profit} \times 100}{\text{Sales}}$$

The 'net profit margin' gives you the picture after taking off your overheads and interest, but before tax.

$$\text{Net Profit Margin} = \frac{\text{Profit before Tax} \times 100}{\text{Sales}}$$

An increasing figure shows a good control of overheads. Here is another useful ratio that measures how productive your business is.

$$\text{Return on Capital} = \frac{\text{Profit before charging Interest and Tax} \times 100}{\text{Total Capital Employed}}$$

5. Some Useful Tips.

Use ratios to examine trends and identify problems. They will never solve problems for you but they might lead you to the cause.

- The smaller the business, the more important it is to watch the cash flow, than just the ratios.
- Ratios depend upon reliable and consistent financial information.
- Remember that ratios are normally judged against 'general business norms' and against the past performance of your business.

APPENDIX E.

APPENDIX E
OPERATING BUDGET.

Business Name

Enter month

Figures rounded to nearest £.	Budget	Actual	Budget	Actual	Budget	Actual	Budget	Actual	Budget	Actual	Budget	Actual	Budget	Actual	Total Budget	Actual
Sales																
1 Cash																
2 Credit																
a Total Sales (1 + 2)																
Variable costs																
3 Goods or materials used																
4 Wages and salaries																
b Total variable costs (3 + 4)																
c Gross profit (a - b)																
d Gross profit as % of sales (c ÷ a x 100)																
Fixed costs																
5 Production/operation																
6																
7																
8																
9																
10																
11 Selling and distribution																
12																
13																
14																
15																
16																
17 Administration																
18																
19																
20																
21																
22																
23 Other expenses																
24																
25																
26																
27																
28																
29 Finance charges																
30 Depreciation																
e Total fixed costs																
f Net profit before tax (c - e)																
g Sales you need to breakeven (e ÷ d x 100)																

Note:
"Goods or materials used" in 3 above is equal to your stock at the start of the relevant financial period, plus what you buy, less the stock you have left at the end of that period.
"Wages and salaries" in 4 includes the wages of workers who make the product or provide the service.

- E 1 -

47

APPENDIX F.

APPENDIX F.
CASHFLOW FORECAST.

Business Name:

Enter month

Figures rounded to £'s | Budget | Actual | Budget | Actual | Budget | Actual | Budget | Actual | Budget | Actual | Budget | Actual | ... | Total Budget | Actual

Receipts
1. Sales (including VAT) - Cash
2. - Debtors
3. Other trading income
4. Loans you have received
5. New capital
6. Selling of assets
7. Other receipts
a. Total receipts

Payments
8. cash for goods you have bought
9. Payments to creditors
10. Owner or directors' withdrawals
11. Wages and Salaries (net)
12. PAYE/NI
13. Capital items (for example equipment and vehicles)
14. Transport and packaging
15. Rent or rates
16. Services
17. Loan repayments
18. Hire or leasing repayments
19. Interest
20. Bank or finance charges
21. Professional fees
22. Advertising
23. Insurance
24.
25.
26. VAT
27. Corporation tax and so on
28. Dividends
b. Total payments
c. Net cashflow (a-b)
29. Opening bank balance
d. Closing bank balance (c ± Line 29)

Basic assumptions - please give details of the assumptions you use when you fill in this form and list any other relevant ones on the next page.

Credit taken - the average time your creditors give you to pay.   Days
Credit given - the average time you give your debtors to pay.   Days

48

APPENDIX G.

FINANCIAL PROBLEM DIAGNOSTIC CHART.

Problem.	Possible causes.	Some remedies.
1. Poor Cashflow.	Lack of sales. Bad debts. Debtors paying late.	See 5 below. See 9 below. Act quickly! Send reminders, make sure the invoice is correct. Carry out credit checks with each new customer or ask for references. Make sure that the terms and conditions on the contract or invoice are clear,
	No system of debt recovery	Ask for professional advice, offer settlement or take legal action.
	Cash tied up in stock	Carry out stock utilisation/turnover check.
2. Cheques bouncing.	Not telling the bank of current circumstances (but see 3 below).	Keep strong control of the bank balance using a daily cash book. Do not pay out until money is in. Tell the bank if you need a temporary overdraft or need to go over your overdraft limit for a short time. Keep strong control of debtors (but see 3 below).

Problem.	Possible causes.	Some remedies.
3. Bank overdraft constantly at the limit.	Taking too much out of the business for your income. Buying capital that should have been funded by a loan. Business is not making a profit. Expanding too much Not controlling debtors. Paying suppliers too quickly. Not monitoring your bank balance. Allowing stocks to grow out of control.	Run monthly accounts. Plan your weekly cashflow. Control your receipts and keep the bank informed.
4. No grants available.	Lack of forward planning. Not keeping in touch with professionals or not getting advice.	Before buying anything significant or expanding, get expert advice on VAT, tax, borrowing and grants.
5. Losses.	Not enough sales. Lack of gross profit because:- * Wrong mix of products or services. * Not putting up price when costs go up. * Theft by employees. * Scrap and waste too high. * Inefficient workforce. * Excessive discounts to customers. * Errors in quotations to customers. * Bad record keeping. * Over valuing your stock. * Margin too low. Costs too high. Costs of expanding and obtaining capital are too expensive in relation to projected sales.	Plan ahead – have a marketing plan and a financial plan. Sell according to planned changes in the market. Monthly accounts should point to what is going wrong. Get specific reports on things like:- * Pricing. * Efficiency of production. * How time is spent. * Scrap and waste. * Quality. Control your costs if they are increasing. If increases are inevitable consider putting your prices up. Consider putting your prices up anyway.

6. High tax bills.	The result of:- * PAYE inquiry. * DTI inquiry. No tax planning. Incorrect methods of buying assets or incorrect timing for buying. Not enough use of pension payments. Becoming a limited company without professional help and planning. Sending forms in late. Not keeping to tax regulations.	Keep all evidence of cheaper sales or events that have affected your gross margin. Take professional advice. Keep good records. Understand tax and obey the rules. Plan your taxes before the end of the year with your professional adviser.
7. High VAT bills.	Result of a VAT inquiry or other tax inquiry. Not keeping to VAT regulations. Using the wrong retail scheme. Sending forms in late. Not giving the right information.	Keep good records. Keep all evidence of cheap sales and things that affect your gross margin. Take advice. Understand the rules and obey them.
8. Increasing personal liability.	Growth. Reduced performance. Continuing to be unprofitable. Lack of financial control.	Consider becoming a limited company, but always take advice. Plan ahead. Have monthly accounts and so on (see 5 above).
9. Bad debts.	Type of industry you are in. No financial control. Not checking out new customers. No continuing check on customers' financial position. No strict system of collecting cash.	Check out all new customers. Have continuing checks on customers' finance. Take out debt insurance. Consider 'debt factoring' (where someone else collects your money). Set up a strict system for collecting cash.

10. High bank charges.	Borrowing over your agreed limit. Using your bank account inefficiently (such as having too many small transaction).	Negotiate with your bank manager. Plan your cash flow. Use your bank account sensibly. Seek the managers' advice on using it better, for example by paying in less cash or by using auto-mated methods of payment.
11. High accountants' fees.	Poor book keeping. Using accountants incorrectly, such as using one when the audit clerk or book keeper would do. Not passing on all the information. Asking for help too late. Not keeping evidence to use in an inquiry.	Get a quotation for every job. Use accountants sensibly. Take advice before making any major business decisions. Keep all evidence.

APPENDIX H.

BREAKDOWN GRAPH

Break-even Analysis (Fibreglass Company).

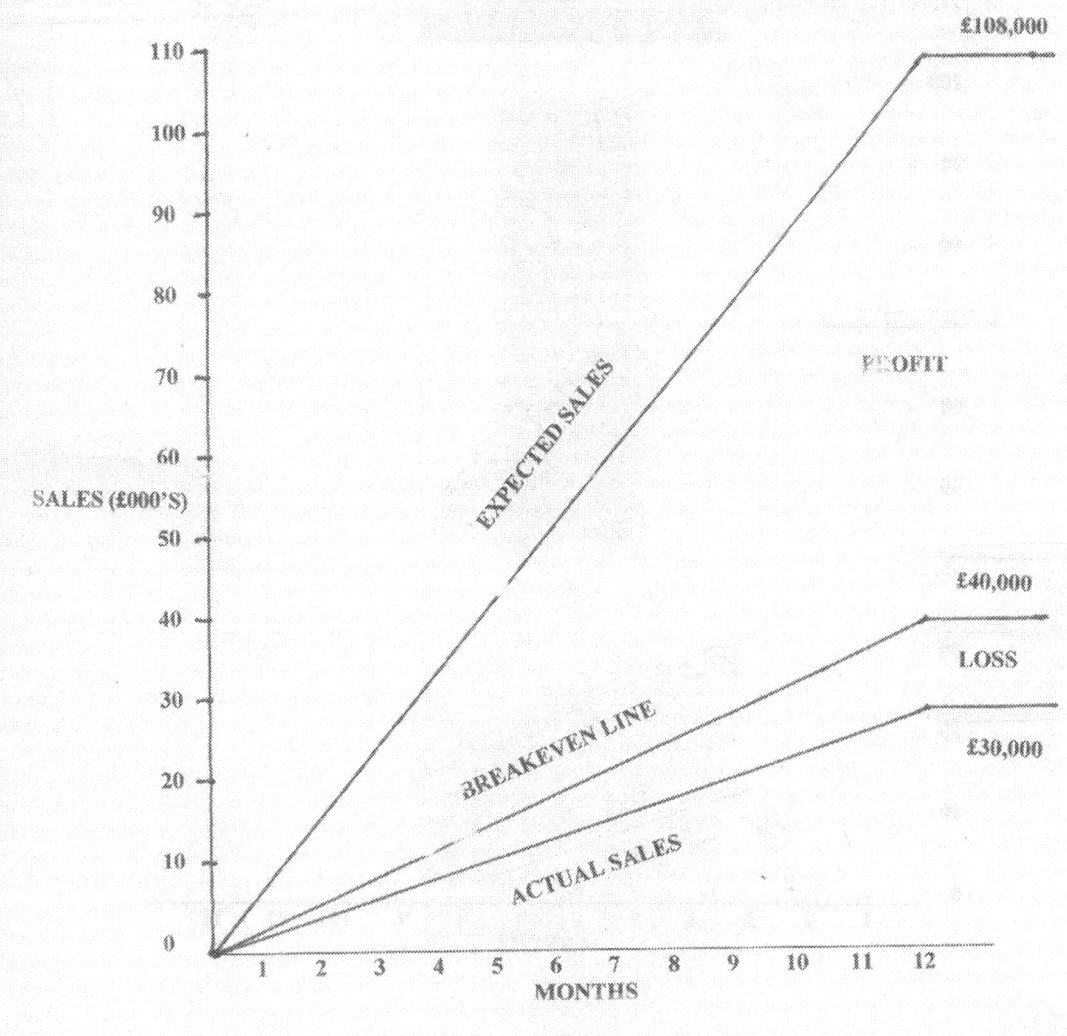

- H 1 -

APPENDIX I.

DEBTOR MATRIX.

Business name:

Amount owing in £'s.

	Debtor.	Total.	Less than 30 days.	30-60 Days.	60-90 Days.	More than 90 Days.
1						
2						
3						
4						
5						
6						
7						
8						
Total						

About the Author

Ian Bell was born at Hastings, England on Christmas Day 1939. He is twice widowed and currently lives in Oldbury-on-Severn near Bristol and is semi retired.

Educated at Chiswick County Grammar school Ian left in 1956 to take up a 5 year apprenticeship as an Aircraft Instrument & Electrical Engineer with British European Airways (BEA).

At the end of his apprenticeship in 1961 he stayed on with BEA for a year working as a Flight Departure Engineer and then followed a series of jobs over the next 35 years. During those years Ian worked as a Technical Author for 5 years and then in Sales & Marketing for 30 years.

During the periods of employment in Sales & Marketing he worked mainly in the Aerospace and Military market sectors with extensive activity in Air, Sea and Land applications of equipments and systems. At one point Ian was based in the USA for 5 years working for Smiths Aerospace as their Harrier (Jump Jet) Programme Manager and then as their Marketing Development Manager. Subsequently he was transferred from the Aerospace side of Smiths back to the Marine Division at Kelvin Hughes at Hainault in England where he remained as their Sales Director for 3 years.

From 1997 Ian has successfully run his own company Berkley Bell Associates which is a Management & Marketing Consultancy having extensive customers both in the UK and overseas.